Oceans of Love: To Us From Us

By

Dee Freeman

To Dwayne,
A Wonderful guy!
Best of luck to you in your travels!
Be Blessed!
Dee Freeman
6/04

1127 Alexandria Drive
Lansing, Michigan 48917
517 321-3122
deekfreeman@aol.com

© 2002 by Dee Freeman. All rights reserved.

No part of this book may be reproduced, stored in a retrieval system, or transmitted by any means, electronic, mechanical, photocopying, recording, or otherwise, without written permission from the author.

ISBN: 1-4033-3779-9 (e-book)
ISBN: 1-4033-3780-2 (Paperback)

This book is printed on acid free paper.

Acknowledgment

This book is especially dedicated to my husband, Myron, who I adore and to whom and for whom I am grateful. He has always been supportive, telling me I could do it. For many years, he has been and remains my number one promoter in all my endeavors.

This work is also dedicated to my loving children, Frederick, Janeece and Myron Jr., and particularly to my grandson, Giovanni, who is my little "Nubian Prince" and who now must bare the weight of holding up his ancestors; to my mother, Beaulah Barnes, who chose me, and was always there for me when I needed a loving helping hand; and to my brother Clarence, who has always boosted my ego by making me feel I can do anything.

I wish to express my appreciation to my family, friends and others of the community who praised my pieces and encouraged me to write this book.

Thanks to all of you, I am now realizing a dream. Oceans of love to all of you.

TABLE OF CONTENTS

ACKNOWLEDGMENT iii

FOLLOWING THEIR LEAD

    INHERITANCE 3
    INFLUENCES 5
    THE JOURNEY 7
    WITHOUT US 9

TOGETHER WE STAND

    TO US FROM US: BLACK LOVE FLOWING 13
    LOVE: IN THE FLESH 15
    SISTAS 17
    LOVE YOUR BLACKNESS 19

RESERVATION…YET WE PRESS FORWARD

    THE QUESTION: WILL THE RING OF FREEDOM
      BRING FREEDOM???? 23
    WHO AM I? 27
    AIN'T I SOMEBODY TOO? 29
    I WEEP 31

GETTING INTO GEAR

    A CHALLENGE: NOW IS THE TIME 35
    WHAT'Z UP YOUNG MAN? 37

GET AN ATTITUDE 39
FREE THE MIND 41
SHOW ME THE MONEY:
    FORTY ACRES AND A MULE 43
WE, AS A PEOPLE, MUST LOVE US 47

A TRIBUTE AND REPORT TO "THE DRUM MAJOR FOR JUSTICE"

STILL, WE WAIT 51
I TOO, DREAM: ODE TO MARTIN 55

OUR FUTURE SEEMS BRIGHT

DOOR OF OPPORTUNITY 61
UPLIFT OUR CHILDREN 63
MY NUBIAN PRINCE 67

DETERMINED TO GO THE DISTANCE

OH FREEDOM 71
YOU GOT POWER, MY BROTHER 73
SOLID IN THE SKIN I'M IN 75
IF NOT YOU, THEN WHO? 79
GONNA MAKE IT 81
FREEDOM: THE PRIZE 85

ABOUT THE AUTHOR 87

INTRODUCTION

"Love is a mighty power, a great and complete good. Love alone lightens every burden, and makes the rough places smooth… Nothing is sweeter than love, nothing stronger, nothing higher, nothing wider, nothing more pleasant, nothing fuller or better in heaven or earth…

Thomas a Kempis,
German Augustinian Monk

Oceans of Love: To Us From Us

FOLLOWING THEIR LEAD

"Every man is a quotation from all his ancestors."

Plato, the philosopher

Dee Freeman

INHERITANCE

Who are you child?
Where do you think you came from?
Are you a proud daughter or are you someone's proud son?
What is your heritage?
What's known about your past?
From where is your lineage flowing?
Does it have strength and fortitude to last?

Do you have the blood in your veins
From the Kings and Queens of your past?
Do you know about your heritage?
Have you taken the time to ask?
I'm advising you to seek out the Elders—
Quiz them, get deep into their mind.
Find out some history and facts about your own proud blood line.

When you've searched the past and found strength,
Wisdom, and knowledge there,
You'll have the foundation that will sustain you,
And take you forward…anywhere.
You'll discover you—
Yes, you - are the benefactor to great and powerful riches.
Its not your nature to bow down to another man,
Nor remain in meager helpless trenches.

Africa's rich culture and art permeates
Through the civilized world today.
It's time we dispelled myths about our heritage,
Let's you and me, lead the way.
Get up child!
Find yourself!
Let's use our minds, our voices and our hands.
Let's make proud our ancestors,
Reclaiming our birthrights inherited from the Motherland.

Dee Freeman

INFLUENCES

I look back and see my people chained and held in bondage against their will. Some were striped of pride, some dignity, some respect, and some even the desire to live.

My people, my people, how proud I am that you had the inner conviction, the strength, the determination and flexibility to survive… the atrocities, the negative influences, the hatred, the indignities, the inhumane acts dumped upon your meager and oppressed lives.

The physical and psychological torture and torment were ills you had to endure. But by grace and will, you made it through. That you kept the faith, walked tall with pride, is an honorable tribute to you, I'm sure.

The influences of a cruel, unjust, and insensitive people have not kept you from the mainstream of life. You continue to show your true character and are rising to great heights in spite of past or present strife.

My people, I am proud to be your heir. I want to uphold your commitment to excellence and make you proud of me too. So I won't allow those negative influences to keep me down. I'll strive, persist, and believe that in the end, I'll make it through.
Just like you.

Dee Freeman

THE JOURNEY

Pained humiliation beset as we were
Snatched from loved ones
Torn from our homeland
Forced onto our first journey
Becoming sometimes our last journey…the dreaded passage

Coffled. Shackled. Deemed cargo.
Forced to accept horrid,
Dehumanizing conditions…
Worth measured only by exchange of copper.

The journey saw us tightly packed.
That horrible hole…incited, uncontrollable rage.
Fury and hatred seeped up from the pits of our hearts.
Salty tears welled in an abominable abyss, then
Rained down from our eyes, to drip and sting our
Bruised, splintered, and withered skin.

This journey towed us over a raging ocean where
Ships tossed and tore our bodies.
Violent waters tormented our viciously violated souls.
Despair, depression, disease, death—
Our constant companions across these cursed waters
That swallowed us by the millions—subtly remain today.
Tarnished waters now hold our ancestors' souls,
Who join hands with those who died before.

Muffled cries from the ocean floor
Call to us. Speaking, voicing their anguish,
Yet sharing their eternal love, strength,
Passion and determination. They tell us…
With the aide of Divine Providence,
We will survive.

Dee Freeman

They whisper words of encouragement.
Their past cleared the way for our future.
Their sacrifice of yesterday paid forward
Our advancement of today.
Their dying enabled our rebirth.

We continue this journey. No longer
Over the oceans, but over the highways of this world;
Over the byways of the minds of people.
We continue the journey of resolve to reclaim our dignity,
Regain our rightful place in a world of continuous movement.

We continue the journey until our ancestors feel
Proud of our accomplishment and our resolution.
We continue, never to turn back.
We'll emerge from the hole,
Undaunted, stronger;
With celebration in our hearts;
Able to sustain any further journey life offers.

Oceans of Love: To Us From Us

WITHOUT US

We shouldered heavy burdens.
With the weight of this Nation on our backs,
We cultivated the lands we could never own.
We've labored and toiled…racked with pain under the man's lash.
We had profound influence in
The development, formation and foundation of this, our nation.
So, tell me, where would this country be, without us?

We laid out cities in spectacular design.
We built the bridges that span large bodies of water.
We separated the plasma from the blood and
Performed the first open heart surgery. Even this feat
Did not soften the hard hearted hatred still
Prevalent in our generation. Our culture has
Been permanently interwoven into the fabric of this nation.
Can you see, where would this country be, without us?

We discovered how to make the first shoes
Hold together and last.
The things Carver did with the peanut is yet,
Believe it or not, unsurpassed.
Even though our blood and sweat are mixed with the mortar of
Great monuments, there is no indication that our people took part
In their construction nor in the formation of the nations' history as it
Stands today.
It's as if we were not worthy of mention.
Heaven forbid we owe any of this nations' splendor to a people of
Such demeaned status.
We are now, however, determined to raise awareness
Of our contributions and participation.
So, do you know where this country would be without us?

Dee Freeman

Our involvement in the common good, the prosperity,
The development, and the economic prowess of this country,
Then and now, hold its fiber together.
Little would exist as it is today had not our blood, sweat, and tears
Gone into the formation of what is now hailed as the world's greatest
Nation.
I shutter to think, where this country would be,
Without us.

Oceans of Love: To Us From Us

TOGETHER WE STAND

"…and no one exists alone; hunger allows no choice
to the citizen or the police; we must love
one another or die."
Wystan Hugh Auden,
British-born American poet

Dee Freeman

TO US FROM US: BLACK LOVE FLOWING

TUFU   To Us From Us—Universal Love

"The greatest of these is LOVE"
Love is our hope
Love renews, it's our healing
Love restores and gives life purpose
Go ahead, feel the feeling.

TUFU   To Us From Us—Self Love

"Love Thyself"
For no one else can do it
Respect yourself, just try it
You'll find - there's nothing to it.

TUFU   To Us From Us—Humankind Love

Give love to someone,
Watch it come right back to ya!
Receive love from someone
Go ahead, believe me, it's due ya!

TUFU   To Us From Us—Family Love

Let us cherish and love each other
Love ourselves, Mother, Father, Sister, Brother
Let us allow the emergence of pure Black-love
To reach heights and depths of that flowing from above.

Dee Freeman

LOVE: IN THE FLESH

She's up before the sun
Undaunted by the pile of tossed
And misplaced curls…some matted
Some dangling
Standing stalwartly looking to the heavens

Daybreak…without fail she braves the newness
She looks back, her mind unfolds the unforgotten
Grief, heartache, suffering
Soon past times become
Clouded by dim visions of the future

She looks ahead, then searches
Her heart for signs of renewal
Of revival
Her faith, her belief, her fortitude
Are all likened to that of an
Old oak tree, standing
Unshakened by the storm

Her precious heart
Pure courage and
Layered experiences
Seem to swell, smooth and soothe the soul
Mending all broken fragments of existence

Giving of herself so completely
She, the keeper of our seed
Vessel of life
Somehow commands will
Commands the very essence of breath
Life…destiny

Dee Freeman

    She hurls rows upon rows of loving supplications
        Which like a spiraling pyramid, ascend
           Each floating upward…skyward
     Meeting in heaven where every single one
      Blends with another to form one of her
  Loving prayers for her family…and the world

SISTAS

I am proud to be ya sista
I am proud to be
Ya confidant and friend
I'll stand by ya side
Be there for ya
Thru the thick and the thin

I'm ya sistah
Ya mother
Ya daughter
I'm ya friend and ya wife
I'm here to share in the highs
And the lows, just any parts
Of ya life

We've come thru hardships
Headaches, heartaches
Rode out the bumps
Of the high roads and the low
Always holding onto
Divine sistahood
We must support each other
Through love, devotion, and
Sincerity, don't cha know

Dee Freeman

Oceans of Love: To Us From Us

LOVE YOUR BLACKNESS

BLACKNESS IS:
B   BOLD, BEAUTIFUL, STRONG, POWERFUL,
      BOUNDLESS AND VERY WISE

BLACKNESS IS:
L   LAVISHED WITH AN AWESOME BLACK LOVE AND
      WITH A SELF ESTEEMING PRIDE

BLACKNESS:
A   ACKNOWLEDGES OUR RICH HERITAGE
      AND ANCHORS US IN A STRONG SENSE OF HISTORY

BLACKNESS:
C   CAPTURES STRENGTH FOR OUR SOULS FROM
      THE OLE WIVES TALES AND THE ANCIENT FOLK STORY

BLACKNESS IS:
K   KNOWLEDGE TO EMPOWER THE PEOPLE-NOT SOME
      BUT THE ENTIRE MASS

BLACKNESS PROCLAIMS:
N   NOW IS THE TIME TO BE STRONGER
      THAN WE EVER WERE IN THE PAST

BLACKNESS MUST:
E   EDUCATE AND TRAIN OUR YOUTH
      SO THAT WE, AS A PEOPLE, WILL LAST

BLACKNESS MUST:
S   SECURE A PLACE IN THE FUTURE FAR BETTER
      THAN THAT GIVEN TO US IN THE YEARS GONE PAST

BLACKNESS HEALS:
S   IT SAVES US FROM THE HALLS OF INJUSTICE;
      SO, LOVE YOUR BLACKNESS AS NEVER BEFORE,
      IT STRENGTHENS OUR GRASP ON EQUALITY;
      AND ALLOWS US TO ENTER THROUGH WISDOM'S DOOR

Dee Freeman

Oceans of Love: To Us From Us

RESERVATIONS…YET WE PRESS FORWARD

"There is no king who has not had a slave among his ancestors, and no slave who has not had a king among his."

Helen Keller,
American writer

Dee Freeman

Oceans of Love: To Us From Us

THE QUESTION: WILL THE RING OF FREEDOM BRING FREEDOM????

Will freedom ever ring from the hills or from the mountain tops of these United States? Will it ever sound loud enough to pay the "Debt" to us, or to even partially compensate? Will it ever flow across the country side like the proverbial milk and honey? Will it ever restore to us our pride, an economic stability, or any compensatory money?

When it rings, will it absolve deeds of omission so that our future can have a creative base from which to pull needed facts? Will this ring of freedom, somehow replicate the missing monuments, legends, statues and documents recorded to leave our legacy in tact? Will the ring of freedom be able to create a secure and prosperous future for a people whose past was taken away? Will it be waved like a magic wand and voila' we'll be equal and have all rights and privileges as others one day?

With the ring of true freedom, will our contributions of the past ever find their way to academia and history books? Will it ever roll around the bends, flow into the valleys, or seep into the desolate crannies and the empty nooks? Will the ring of freedom revitalize our smothered memories of the stolen history of our past? Will freedom ring to set us free and tell the world the whole truth, nothing but the truth at last? When will it ring?

Can this ring at last erase the blasphemous and vicious connotations written by the founding fathers and the likes? Will freedoms' ring abate suffering, even as you read this, that has been passed down through generations of strife? Can this ring of freedom overshadow this inhumane, slanderous and character demeaning plight? When freedom rings to free us at last, will it ring without an assaulting and bloody fight?

When freedom rings, will it finally unveil the horrifically brutal and massive crimes of bondage against us? When these freedom bells toll, will they fall on deaf ears or will there be noble people in charge whom we can trust? Will it uncover the lies, the half truths, and deceits that now unfurl our story? Will it somehow catapult us to our rightful position to receive proper due and a glimpse of pride and glory?

Will Freedoms' ring ever work on the minds of those who ultimately enslaved us? Will it ever speed up its' cure so as to aide and to help save us? Will it break open the shackles, and free us of the vicious racism or cruel strife? Will it ever ring true, giving us back our pride, our dignity, and our precious fleeting life? When will freedom ring?

Can this ring of Freedom bring back my people, whom this wretched inhumanity has willingly slain? Will the ring ever dull the hurt of losing a loved one. Oh, will it stop the pain? Will the cry of freedom and lamentations of my ancestors go unanswered, unnoticed and unheard? When freedom finally rings for us, will it be more than a mere empty word?

Will that ring soften the bites of the dogs that were made to chase us? Will it lessen the sting of the water jets that hit us and abased us? Will this ring of freedom ever begin to justify how and why it is only Africa's past that is always lost? When it rings, can I put my faith into the fact we'll get the straight forward facts at any cost?

Will Freedom ever ring out and give us what everyone knows is rightfully due us? Will it ever grow fast enough to help emancipate, elevate and imbue us? Will the ring of Freedom allow America to share with us her monetary and economic gains? Will this freedom be able to return to us our dignity lost under immeasurable shame?

When Freedom rings, will it retrieve the memories of times when we were once great? Will it bring back to us that knowledge of a lost self at this late date? Will we ever know Freedom as it was in Ancient times of Timbuktu? Will the truth of our heritage and our greatness ever get back to me and you?

When Freedom rings, will it pull up the lost history of our royalty, being descendant of Queens and Kings? Will the ring of Freedom allow our stories to tell the whole truth, about a whole bunch of things? Will it ever be spoken truthfully by the "Man" and allowed to be printed in his press? Will it ever evolve to lift us up, for we are still so unequivocally oppressed? When will freedom ring?

Will the ring of freedom silence the chants of old-"you're chattel...go back to Africa...where you belong?" Will this ring make it plain what we're about, where we're headed, and how we can all just get along? Will freedoms' ring wake up the fact that we as a nation, have been grossly wronged? Will this ring of freedom bring about a change in us so we'll be able to unite and become strong?

Can this ring of freedom, ever finally be the saving grace we pray will soon unfurl? Will this ring tell the true story of our contributions to this whole blessed world? Will it expound on the long past social, economic and political systems that were extensively developed? Can this freedom elevate our people out of the mire and stigmas within which we are so often enveloped? When will freedom ring?

Well, I for one want freedom to ring, for now is the time. For when it rings, I want you and me to be around to hear the melodious chime. I want it to ring long, to ring loud, and to ring all around the country side. Then we, as a people, will all share the much needed and long awaited racial pride.

Dee Freeman

Oceans of Love: To Us From Us

WHO AM I?

Jesse Jackson tells me "I am somebody"
Michael Jackson sings "I'm the one in the Mirror"
Maya Angelou says I'm a
"Phenomenally Phenomenal Woman"

Yet I despair
Is it because I still hear the voices of the
Former slave owners saying that
I am only two-thirds of a citizen?

Aretha Franklin bellows, I should demand
"Respect"
The Staple Singers vocalizes I should
"Respect Myself"
Helen Baylor melodically croons "I've got the Victory" and I agree

So why do I despair?
Why am I despondent?
Is it because
I can't seem to find my right place in society?

My friends say I'm gifted and talented
My husband tells me I'm his beauty queen
My history & heritage bequeaths that
I'm a descendant of Kings and Queens

Yet, I have doubts
That surface and rob me of fully
Realizing
And appreciating my self worth

Dee Freeman

Martin Luther King, Jr. shouts from the mountain top
That "I'm free at last"
Malcolm X proclaimed
I have now and have always had "Black Power"
James Brown bellows I should
"Say it loud, I'm Black and I'm Proud"
The Holy Word gently reminds me
That I am a child of the King

So, I look in the mirror
Then delve deep within myself
There I see the birth of a New ME!
A brand New ME

Now I See Who I Am
Now I can sing!
Now I can shout to the world!

Now I can stand tall
Yell it from the mountain tops!
Now I can walk proudly, with my head held high
Now I know that I AM SOMEBODY!

The reflection in the mirror is ME!
I AM ME!
And "I Gotta be me"
I am an intelligent creation of the Almighty
I am a PROUD African-American!
I am a PROUD Black WOMAN

Who has found self-love
The awesome power of Black Love
Opens like a cocoon and awakens my spirit
It transforms me into
The real me, I truly long to be

Oceans of Love: To Us From Us

AIN'T I SOMEBODY TOO?

SAY, What are you thinking, and can you tell me why
Those thoughts are running through your mind?
I can surmise from the look on your face,
What you're thinking about me is not very kind.

Hold on now, just think about this life,
God made me and the same God made you,
So why you think you're better than me?
Ain't I Somebody Too?

Your look is conveying dislike. Are you thinking
That I should not be here?
Your glare, frown, and the shake of your head
Awaken in me a once dreadful fear.

Take a minute now, and just look at yourself,
Who the h_ _ _ gave all the power on earth to you?
I was placed here as well, and I will no longer be denied,
What do you think now, Ain't I Somebody Too?

You always belittle me with your cruel words,
Speaking them without giving much thought.
Saying how things should still now be
The same as when I was sold and bought.

Hey, let's look at things from my perspective;
The constitution says I am equal to you.
Just give me my inalienable rights, I deserve them now,
For, I know, I Am Somebody Too!!

Dee Freeman

I WEEP

I WEEP for myself
    For my children
    For my ignorance of self
I weep sadly, for I feel I can do nothing else

I weep for my Ancestors
    For their suffering
    For their dying
I weep freely, not knowing why I'm crying

I weep for those who know nothing
    of their heritage
    For those who don't even care
I weep in silence, in solace, and sometimes in despair

I weep for my people
    For my country
    For my nation
I weep while I lay here—too soul weary, too patient

I weep for us all now
    For the future
    For eternity
    For the past
I weep deeply, hoping the hurt will soon pass

Dee Freeman

Oceans of Love: To Us From Us

GETTING INTO GEAR

"…why should we be cowed (scared) by the name of action? …We know the ancestor of every action is thought…to think is to act."

Ralph Waldo Emerson,
American poet

Dee Freeman

A CHALLENGE: NOW IS THE TIME

The challenge is to:
Raise our awareness, raise our expectation
Keep our demands in the forefront of the Nation

Break free from the shackles of all type prejudice
Regenerate and rejuvenate a bold stance for equal justice

Close the ever widening economic gap
Snap out of the teeth of the Slavery Trap

Stress the issues of complete racial equality
Remove the stigmas of racial inferiority

Think out of the "box". Find our loud voice
Create some prosperous strategy, with unlimited choice

Gather our voices and energize our political clout
Let's get on the move. Simply put, get the lead out

Stop the slow moral and social declines
Upgrade and energize the wasting, stagnant minds.

Loosen our minds from the harsh psychological constraints
Find the real truth, for sometimes reality may appear what it ain't

Educate the masses, learn of and treasure our history
Take control of our destiny and heal our scarred dignity

Elevate our selves from the mire of the bottomless pit
Wake up and unite. Get up and get on with it

Dee Freeman

Wake up from intellectual abuse
Stop the dying from excess drug misuse

Bolster self-esteem and show self love
Ask for guidance and power from above

Light a heated fire under your seat and mine
Get up and get cracking, for now is the time.

Oceans of Love: To Us From Us

WHAT'Z UP YOUNG MAN?

NOW is the time YOUNG MEN

NOW is the time

Now IS the T I M E

WAKE UP   GET UP   LISTEN UP

SIT UP   STRAIGHTEN UP

PULL UP   STAND UP

The world won't stand still for you! It must keep moving forward. YOU must WAKE UP!

Time is no longer awaiting. You need to get busy! You should GET UP!

Knowledge is the key to success. Educators are trying to help you. So why don't you LISTEN UP?

There are role models enough out there. Just look around. Be attentive and SIT UP!

You have the opportunity to achieve greatness if you'd only apply your talents. Change your attitude and STRAIGHTEN UP!!

Take pride in your appearance. Dress with more dignity. Get a belt and PULL UP!!

Become the MAN we know you can be. The future is depending on you. Hold your head high and STAND UP!!

Dee Freeman

Oceans of Love: To Us From Us

GET AN ATTITUDE

Pride is an attitude - believe it or not,
        And <u>we</u> have a right to be PROUD
Don't be timid - let's declare it again
        Say it with strength and say it LOUD.

We are the heirs of ROYALTY
        LETS' WALK the walk to show our pride.
We can overcome the bonds of adversity
        LETS' TALK the talk—we have nothing to hide.

Show our true colors of RED, BLACK AND GREEN
They represent a tradition we must hold dear and cherish.
    We must learn from our past, to never let our guard down
Against those who would see us perish.

If we think it, we can achieve it
    Go for the gusto, we C A N overcome the toils and strife
We have the knowledge of the past, and the wisdom of the future
    Together these can produce a focused and productive life.

We must adopt that CAN do, M U S T do now attitude
We can't wait for others to do this for us
We are a proud people with a strong will for survival
We <u>can </u>do it, as God shields the way before us.

Through the years-with God-we've come a <u>long way</u>!
So, press onward, look to the almighty, and give Him sincere gratitude. It's our duty to WALK TALL—
Holding our heads high, for we're endowed with great pride and a rewarding and positive attitude.

Dee Freeman

FREE THE MIND

Free the mind
    Free the man
    Loosen the chains on
    His self motivation

Free the mind
    Free the man
    Unleash his pent up and
    Trodden aspirations

Free the mind
    Free the man
    To uphold freedom, liberty
    And justice for all

Free the mind
    Free the man
    To rise up with a powerful answer
    To desperations call

Free the mind
    Free this man
    To no longer surrender to
    Shackles on ankle, mind, and hand

Free the mind
    Of our new free men
    And they will rise up
    To take a united stand.

Dee Freeman

Oceans of Love: To Us From Us

SHOW ME THE MONEY: FORTY ACRES AND A MULE

Where is the restitution that's our due…
The reparation and debt
Owed to me and you?

For hundreds of years
We've been born into poverty.
Over those same years we've
Endured unimaginable iniquity.

We now barely eke out a decent living.
From the beginning,
It's always been us who's been giving.
We don't always know where we came from.
We're often unstable,
We drift; we then settle for the slum.

We don't know where
We've been or even
Where we're going.
We check out the crystal ball,
But don't know what it's showing.

We don't know of our past Royalty.
We often practice disloyalty.
We've been known to
Disrespect each other;
Our mother, our father,
Our sister, and our brother.

So, to get us back onto
The right upward mobile tracks,
We need what's due us
To support the heavy load
Placed upon our backs.

Dee Freeman

We never got the promised land.
When we did, many times, it was just sand.
We never got the promised mule.
Only promises, more promises,
Many making us out to be the fool.

They say help yourself, but
We had no bootstraps to pull ourselves up.
Now we bite the bullet
Sipping slowly from a full bitter cup.

We toil for the man,
Seemingly unceasingly.
We're jailed by the man,
Noticeably increasingly.

We can't seem to get a head,
We most often have to rent.
We can't seem to save money.
None; not a single red cent.
We endure a world of sadness and gloom.
We often suffer and sometimes
Feel we're doomed.

We meander through life
In severe hopelessness.
We may even die
Broke; many times homeless.

But, with all these things
Working to keep us down.
We somehow endure and
Live life, seldom with even a frown.

Oceans of Love: To Us From Us

We now, again, ask for the
Reparation that is our due,
So we may build a life
And dwell in this existence anew.

So, show me the money…
The forty acres and a mule,
We'll use them to lift ourselves;
Our long awaited well-defined tool.

Dee Freeman

Oceans of Love: To Us From Us

WE, AS A PEOPLE, MUST LOVE US

We, as a people, are Black, Beautiful, Proud,
Diverse and Intelligent.

    We have much to offer and through continued struggles,
    have given much to this country and the world.

    So, let us celebrate and show love to each other. We must see more love and beauty in ourselves and others, and with a song in our hearts, we can and will prevail.

We, as a people, have contributed much, and have done so with unrestrained integrity.

    We were stolen away from our Mothers and Fathers.
    We survived the catastrophic oppression, and many times
    thrived spiritually in yesteryear's system that put our mental
    and physical being under assault.

We, as a people, were physically contained by outward restraints, but soared mightily through a plethora of inner strength.

    We were forced under the lash to labor long and hard for others, but were also able to provide numerous materialistic contributions to this land.

We, as a people, have been forced to give of ourselves-mentally, physically, and psychologically-but, have retained our determination, our ethnicity, and our pride.

    We therefore deserve all the Love that we give to ourselves.
    The Black Love that only we can give. For if we don't, who will?

We, as a people, have had the physical shackles removed from our ankles, now it is time we remove them from our minds.

> We must stand tall and bold, letting the world know "We are Somebody!" and are equals in the sight of God, even if not to other men.

We, as a people, must continue to advocate the strengths and bonds formed in the past as well as those newly recognized.

> We must respect our aged and ourselves; we must reinforce our efforts to teach, to lead, and to love our youth. Give to them and to each other The Black Love that is TUFU. TO US FROM US!!

We, as a people, must generate ideas to improve our situation while holding on to our ideals, culture, and heritage.

> We cannot leave to history, science, sociology, politics, economics, or chance, the obligation to acquaint the world with our story. We must step forward and do this ourselves; being persistent, even if it means getting an attitude.

We, as a people, have had many in the past to help bare our burdens and our crosses.

> We now have to search deep within our own souls and resources and find the courage to shoulder these pains and hardships; and find the solutions that are needed to propel us to a victorious station.

We, as a people, have the faith and fortitude, the head and heart, the potential and power, the stamina and substance, the tenacity and toughness, and the will and wisdom to come together and make this a better world.

> We, as a people, must love US.
> We must give Hope.
> We must appreciate our Ethnicity.
> Only, we have that Awesome power to give Black Love
> TUFU - To Us From Us.

Oceans of Love: To Us From Us

A TRIBUTE AND REPORT TO "THE DRUM MAJOR FOR JUSTICE"

"Truth is the summit of being; justice is the application of its affairs."

Ralph Waldo Emerson,
American poet

Dee Freeman

STILL, WE WAIT

During the Civil Rights struggle, our Drum Major for justice, Dr. King said "we've suffered injustice for years." I agree, yes, we've suffered and have shed far too many tears. We've been told to wait, to be patient, just hold on. No one denies we've waited, but I ask, why must we have to wait so long? Even though many civil rights victories have been accomplished, we wait for ultimate equality to surface, to take a united stand. Justice has yet to become a reality for all, and I yearn to see Lady Liberty offer this fairness through out the land.

Dr. King said "Justice too long delayed is Justice denied". He asked "How long will prejudice blind the vision of men?" I now join with him by saying…"Not Long". Though we have yet to overcome evil and adversity, we shall never give in. Many years have passed and some of us still wait, right here on the brink of justice, freedom and equality. One hundred thirty nine (139) years after the signing of The Emancipation Proclamation, we still wait for the removal of invisible shackles from you and me.

We wait for our Nation to make real their promises of unobstructed justice, as this is where it should begin. Still, we wait to be judged by the content of our character rather than by the color of the skin we're in. We wait for the power structures that be, to take full responsibility for political stagnation, replacing all backward movement, with a forward, progressive and unified Nation. We wait for justice and righteousness to roll down like that mighty stream and the blending of the melting pot to reach the evolution of Dr. King's dream.

We are here Dr. King, seeking a real order of justice and yes, we still wait. We're not leaving, nor giving up - for the Liberty Bell can never ring too late. We wait, for we have a vested interest in this our country. We've labored here, hard and long. This nation was built upon our backs, which may now be bent, but are yet proud, powerful and strong.

Dee Freeman

We do realize: Our search for freedom has eluded us and our thirst for justice has gone unquenched, yet we go on waiting. We pursue the eradication of racism and drink from the fountain of possibilities, as we go on waiting. We wait even though our suffering, pain and heartaches have brought many tears. We wait even though our request for restitution has fallen onto deaf ears, We patiently wait even though our quest for knowledge has taught us many lessons. We wait even though our tenacity has enabled us to overcome catastrophic oppressions.

Still, we wait for:
    The return of our stolen history
    The return of our precious human dignity
    An apology that we have been grossly wronged
    A change to bring about unity to make us strong

Thou we still wait, Dr. King, we now feel your "urgency of the moment". We incessantly express, as you did 34 years ago, our utter discontent. We wait, and resolve as you, that
Now is the time for equality to flow into the valleys,
Around the bends, and up the meandering mountain side.
Now is the time we work to "speed up that day"
That freedom rings, so we'll impart long awaited pride.
Now's the time to put substantial fervor back into our quest.
Now is the time for vigorous action, giving only our best.
Now's the time for the forces of justice to rise up and become clear.
Now's the time all forms of oppression are ended; words I long to hear.
Now is the time to gather momentum and be bold.
Now is the time, our own destiny, we take total control.
Now is the time we mold into racial harmony, rising to the top.
Now is the time that we-committed to the struggle-have no plans to stop.
Now is the time to retrieve liberty and justice for which we all long.
Now is the time to let freedom ring as it peals out a brand new song.
Now is the time for a belated and glorious transformation.
Now's the time equality emerges from the entrails of this our exalted Nation.

Oceans of Love: To Us From Us

We, as a people, wait. We'll never give up, and are determined never to be turned around. We will continue to move forward until justice and authentic equality resound.

Dr. King, we are wordless to express our gratitude, you dedicated your all for our struggle…giving the ultimate sacrifice.

You freely gave for the cause; your time, your heart, and most precious, you gave your life.

So, we, like you, years later continue:
    to struggle,
    to seek fulfillment of our Forefathers promises,
    to pray fervently-eyes
    to the majestically rolling hill.

For until that day, when all God's children can walk in peace times, shoulder to shoulder, receiving equality and justice, Dr. King, We wait, still.

Dee Freeman

I TOO, DREAM: ODE TO MARTIN

I too dream that we, as a people, will surely rise. Rise to the top, as cream rises, for we have too long been on the bottom of life's totem pole. We can rise, if each one will reach one - if each one will teach one - and if each one will lift another to the level and status we know we must all reach-being inextricably intertwined, if we, as a nation are to truly rise.

I too dream that we, as a people, will elevate ourselves to meet the challenges set before us by those insensitive to and uncaring of our needs. I dream we will continue to overcome the oppressions caused by racism, Jim Crowism, exploitation and disenfranchisement. This hasn't been an easy task, but we now have more resources, around which we must unite. We now recognize more opportunities, so I implore you to persevere, dig deep, buckle down, get on with it, knuckle down, hop to it and just do it. Dr. King I Too Dream!!

I too dream that we will soon "break loose from the shackles of prejudice..." I dream that someday, there will be no need for our children to be comforted by the words of a loving parent, 'honey, you are as good as anyone else,' because there will no longer be a concept of subservience or inferiority for us, as a people. For this misplaced label will have long been squelched, uprooted, demolished, and displaced. I dream that we won't let the half truths, that flow from forked tongues of those yet untouched by God, keep us down, nor will we let those half truths impede our forward thrust to full and total equality. I dream we will rekindle our quest for equality. We will get back on the right track - headed in the right direction; and led by the Grace of God, we'll be transformed into a blessed and prosperous nation of people of which we can all be proud to be a part. Our charge is to imbue the minds of our youth, build an unshakeable foundation, instill and firmly implant within them the urgency and the need for creative, positive and prompt action. We must let them know that their heritage is a great legacy and let them know that only through them, will we continue to be the proud and beautiful people that is our destiny. For Dr. King, I Too Dream!

Dee Freeman

I too dream that if we, as a people, will all pull together, we can prevent the continuous decline and deterioration of our morals, our values, and our sense of dignity for self. I dream we will be able to conquer our weaknesses, fears, and most obstacles placed to hinder us. We'll be able to look uncertainty, indecisiveness, and every single challenge straight in the eye. I too dream that we won't allow the stigma of ignorance, with which we've been so casually characterized, to interfere with our show of intelligence, impede our acquisition of higher education, or fester and taint our inner concept of self worth. I dream that we will soon begin to hold our heads high. We will strengthen our capability to unite. We'll connect and bind. We'll join together, we'll come together, we'll bond together, and we'll support each other, so that we can become that LOUD voice to be heard and reckoned with - as should have been our unquestionable and inalienable rights from birth. Yes Dr. King, I Too Dream!!

I too dream that we, as a people, will make the necessary sacrifices to ensure that we all have:
> Food enough to feed our bodies—Education enough to enrich our minds—Dignity enough to hold high our heads—Spirituality enough to encourage the soul—Equality enough to rejuvenate our spirits—Justice enough to calm our sense of injustice—and, Freedom enough to bring to fruition all of our heartfelt dreams.

For with our cultural identity intact, our renewed vision secured, we'll press forward to a dauntless and encouraging future and we will reach the promise land. Yes, Dr. King, I Too Dream!!!

I too dream that one day, we won't have to have laws to make others respect us as individuals. We won't have to have laws to say we can now be counted as full human beings. And oh yes, our votes will be counted, whenever and wherever they're cast, not discarded at the whim and discretion of others. I dream we will share equal rights and have all privileges as every other creed and race of this nation. I TOO DREAM, 'WE'LL HAVE EQUALITY'. I dream our voices will be clearly heard-not muffled. I dream our contributions will be fully acknowledged and have their places in history-not partially accredited to us and shared by others or even yet, not noted at all. I dream the vast hues of our skin will no longer be a distraction, will no longer determine our social status, will no longer cause negative reactions. But, these beautiful and varied hues will be recognized as the base of the Rainbow, and as the heart of the Melting pot of this great Nation. I dream we will all be members of a unified and caring Human Race, and we'll be accepted, yes, fully accepted as God has always intended.

Dr. King left us with a great legacy. He did his best to show us the Way!! I dream we'll soon pull it all together, and make him proud of us one day! We'll hold on to our heritage and onto our cultural identity; following his lead and rising majestically to the top; that's when we'll undoubtedly be free. We'll then say with deep conviction & resolve; we'll say with solemn pride…this meaning will ring true; it'll ring loud and it'll ring wide!!! Its message will ring, echo and vibrate like a mighty thunderous Blast!! For Dr. King, I too dream that one day, we'll be "Free at last."

We can all say it proudly "Free at last. Free at last. Thank God Almighty, We're free at last."
What is your Dream?

Dee Freeman

Oceans of Love: To Us From Us

OUR FUTURE SEEMS BRIGHT

"Brightness of our future shines because we, as individuals, possess the capacity to want better, do better, become better; therefore we see the light of faith and soar toward the very stars."

Dee Freeman,
Poet, writer

Dee Freeman

DOOR OF OPPORTUNITY

You don't have to accept this barrier or
Condition you feel you've run into
Or when things aren't going your way
And you don't know
Just what to do
Look at your obstacle, scrutinize and search it completely through
Then look to God for guidance
He'll provide a clear path for you

There is always a way - where there's a will to succeed
There's a supernatural strength that comes—
When you're in desperate need

Ralph Waldo Emerson says it best, "…there's a door in every wall…"
Also, Our Heavenly Father says He'll help you, all you need do is call
The door won't always be obvious when
You're pressed against that wall
You'll have to turn and look for the opening
Which may be ever so small

For many of us, walls and obstacles seem always to dun our path
We must have heart, faith, courage, strength
And endurance to make us last
We must also do our part to help create this escaping door
By preparing ourselves—
Wanting and striving always-to do a little bit more

There will be high walls, low walls
Many walls of immeasurable sizes
We must never succumb to these barriers that rob us
Of a wealth of prizes
Some walls we encounter
Have been passed down through the ages
Together we must chip away at them
Even if only in small groups and stages

Dee Freeman

Each wall offers a door of opportunity
To grow and move on toward success
If we fight a good fight and open the door
We'll come through it being our best

UPLIFT OUR CHILDREN

From the depths of my soul, a voice emerges,
With every breath, I listen and soon hear a gift
An enlightened message that reveals our future evolves…
Only when our precious
Children we uplift.

Our parents made marks on our lives that
Will never be forgotten nor will they ever be erased
Our children, with constant nurturing, will excel in the days ahead
And overcome most challenges
For which they might be faced.

Our forefathers, our roots, affirm, you and I are the proud
Product of their past deeds
Our impending world will spring forth
From our children, who are our sprouting and developing seeds.
Looking back, I see clearly that our survival depends
Upon our forging ahead
For it is by the hands of the innocent,
I'm told, we shall all be led.

As we seek the future
Increased parental participation,
Improved educational equality,
Involvement of church and
Community are vitally essential
We can't move forward to achieve our dreams,
Unless we motivate,
Then cultivate,
The attributes of our children's potential.

Dee Freeman

Our ancestors, upon whose shoulders we stand, cry out
Their pleas float from the ocean floor,
They urge us to encourage and support our children
For they know to move forward,
We must use the opportunity locked behind every door.

We must provide knowledge and know how
Build character, create positive attitudes,
Offer wisdom, comfort and love
We owe this devotion to our children,
As we all rely on the loving
Benevolence of our heavenly Father above.

So, as a village, I implore, let's bond together now
Initiate a call to action, and solemnly vow,
To "Uplift your child, uplift my child at every juncture ".
At every stage and
Phase of their precious lives
Uplift them at any time, on any occasion
At every chance we get, 24/7/365.

Our responsibility to our species is to make our youth
Safe, strong, successful;
Because
Whatever we hope to harvest
From what our tomorrows will bring,
Will depend largely upon our collective
Teaching,
Coaching,
Tutoring,
Nurturing,
Loving,
And uplifting of our ever maturing offspring.

Oceans of Love: To Us From Us

So to our children
Our offspring, our youth,
Our intelligent and loving heirs,
Go forward in love,
Go forward in peace,
And Go with God, who truly cares.

Dee Freeman

Oceans of Love: To Us From Us

MY NUBIAN PRINCE

My prince, you are royalty
Although you may not sit high on any throne
You have an ability to command many to follow
Your lead, even though many times you
May go the distance alone.

Your attire, My Prince, may not be purple
Or silk or come close to that worn by a
Royal family. But the majestic inner aura and
Regal attitude you depict, brings honor and
Respect from and to us, your loyal family.

It's not hard to see, My Prince, that you possess
A rare quality. You personify dignity and
Pride. You make us proud to be your sister,
Daughter, mother, or soul mate walking
Here by your side.

Prince, My magnificent Nubian Prince, we hail you,
Holding you high with love and undying esteem…
You are, as are we all, from greatness;
Exemplifying nobility flowing through us—
Heirs of great Kings and Queens.

Nubian Prince, there's no need to search for our
Identity. We know exactly what and who we are.
We need only to keep walking tall, eyes to the sky,
We'll, no doubt, seize that "unreachable star".

Dee Freeman

Oceans of Love: To Us From Us

DETERMINED TO GO THE DISTANCE

"When a thing is done again and again, it seems to proceed from a deliberate judgment of reason…"

St. Thomas Aquinas,
Scholastic philosopher

Dee Freeman

OH FREEDOM

To our bitter dismay, you're yet elusive
For years, we sought to conquer the fight
To capture the victory you shield from view
And hold just beyond our grasp…out of sight

Your challenge, heated with contempt
Your hurled anger of a darker hue
You've slept through out time
Letting nightmares rise from your REM
Aiding hatred, destruction and death…
Destroying our peace of mind

Freedom, awaken post haste
Surface afresh and breathe anew
Our heavy burden-lift them up high
Open up to authentic peace and goodwill
Set our spirit and being free
Our soul…set free…to fly

Oh freedom, can you comfort us?
Will you embrace us?
Will you, with eagerness protect us?
Will you bring us from darkness
Set us into the marvelous light
Or remain elusive to again reject us?

When we call upon you, Oh Freedom
Bring us deliverance, honor and our natural birth right
Bring us hope, a peace and universal love
A future that will radiate exceptionally bright

Dee Freeman

Destroy the shackle encasing our minds
Update and renovate our splendid history
We await the promise of triumphant…
We await your…Victory

Freedom…Oh Freedom!!

Oceans of Love: To Us From Us

YOU GOT POWER, MY BROTHER

A million Black men came together,
To demonstrate togetherness and unity.
Their mission: To direct positive power and love
For one another, when they returned to their community.

You Got Strength, My Brother, unleash it now,
Don't dare waste another hour.
You have the victory within your grasp, look inside
And realize your God given power.

You Got Motivation from Jesse, Barry,
Maya, and Lewis, just to name a few.
They added great depth and meaning to your day
But the hero, My Brother, is YOU!

You are the cornerstone of our world
Providing the needed love, honor and respect.
Use that strength and power, whenever and wherever needed,
Because you've got your families,
Homes and futures to protect.

You got power - Don't be afraid to unleash it;
Go on and use it this very hour.
It's up to you -Are you up to it?
Use it now,
Don't lose that dynamic Beautiful Black Power.

When you use the power properly,
It has great range.
Employ it and retrieve from the world your fair share.
Show them all…
That your strength makes you no longer
Dependent on this man's welfare.

Dee Freeman

By unleashing the power,
My proud Black Brother,
The world's riches are at your call and command.
So with your love, ability, determination, and power to uplift—
Your collective strength will
Enable our people to stand.

SOLID IN THE SKIN I'M IN

Although I'm always physically,
emotionally,
and spiritually making and remaking me,
I keep trying relentlessly to connect,
to redefine,
even redesign inner self,
I am proud to be who I am—
Proud to be here—
Proud to be me.

Some times I feel
my entire consciousness
seeks the worlds' acceptance of who I am—
the me I've become.
Why do I care
or desire such acceptance,
I ask?
What's hidden deep in my
unconscious self?

Do I somehow feel this way
because my psyche
has not yet evolved
beyond the Willie Lynch theory
that plays with my head;
keeping me thus forever
enslaved?

Dee Freeman

Just
at that lowest point,
there's a power surge.
An eruption, a gush,
an outpouring and an ultimate overspill
of my will to triumph
over such a state of mind,
keeping me ever motivated to be
the best me I can be.

I therefore
emerge
with the aid of my
Omnipotent God.
I emerge
from that deep obscurity.
I emerge
to summon up my true inner might
and deal with being real in
this, the skin I'm in.

Still storms rage periodically,
so I'm often laboring
to quiet the tempest
that seethes within.
I look for the fuse of inspiration
to ignite it,
thereby subjugating any other
smoldering disturbance.

Searching,
probing,
and penetrating deep inside,
in solitude,
I acquire sustenance that in some way
has been
molded,
sculptured,
embedded
into my being and it,
it alone creates what could be,
from what is.

So, even though
I sometimes descend
into the seemingly bottomless pit,
and I wonder,
speculate,
and question what's going on
without and within,
I never demean or doubt myself.
I simply meditate on what I know
as my reality
and feel secure
to be in the skin I'm in.

Dee Freeman

Although
I work at keeping
the outer me radiant and youthful,
healthy and appealing,
there are times I must put forth even greater efforts
to love me as
I am;
my whole self,
my total person,
my entire being…
That is me, myself and I.

My whole being, my body,
my mind, my consciousness,
my soul,
my spirit,
my divine force,
my essence
and my core,
all share this space.

So we,
the Trinity and me,
sharing this space,
this time and place,
are proud to be genuine,
firm and solid in this
"the skin I'm in."

Oceans of Love: To Us From Us

IF NOT YOU, THEN WHO?

Are you leading, standing, following or
Are you just there in the way?
Do you babble something negative when you talk,
Or do you have something of importance to say?

      Are you helping to lift someone up?
      How often do you lend a helping hand?
      Do you block progress by stalling and procrastinating,
      Or are you the one taking a negative stand?

Who are you? What's your role, your vision?
Can you see why you've been put here?
I believe you now have a chance to do something good
In life, something honorable, so take heart and be sincere.

      You can become that leader—
      For good men and women are
      Increasingly hard to find.
      This is a challenge for you.
      If not you, then who?
      Come on now!
      Make up your mind.

You don't have to sit idle, nor follow the crowd.
There is much work in this world that you can do.
The challenge is - Get busy leading now.
The Where and the How—
God has left up to YOU!!!

Dee Freeman

Oceans of Love: To Us From Us

GONNA MAKE IT

Because of the strong backs and shoulders of our ancestors and the bridges made by their sweat and toils, we can stand here today, tall and with our shoulders squared and our eyes to the sky…knowing we're gonna make it.

We need to look at ourselves:
> Scrutinize what we're doing to ourselves
> Make every effort to take care of ourselves
> Look deep within and know ourselves
> Open up our hearts and love ourselves
> Yet know, we're gonna make it

We stand on the strong shoulders of the fore runners of great families, which are still today, as they were in the past, as solid as the rock of Gibraltar. We will no longer sit down idly and let others abuse us.

Lets all put these negative experiences we've encountered into perspective; using them as lessons learned; using them as building blocks to inspire, uplift, enlighten and encourage our spirits to forge ahead to new heights.

Let's use these age old struggles and painful experiences to catapult us to new pinnacles of success and to peak plateaus of life. From this view I can clearly see that we've come a long way, and even though we have further to go, we're gonna make it.

Standing on the shoulders of my Ancestors allows me to:
> See beyond the deliberate debasement of the Bell Curve
> See over the humiliation, connotations and implications of segregation
> Disregard the blatant racism that's yet surging uncontrollably in the urban cities

Dee Freeman

From up here the vision points to a true freedom and equality that we've yet to encounter
        We shall soon go through the fire, and come through tempered, complete and sparkling
        On the wings of love and knowledge, we'll soon soar to a new summit

From up here I can see above and beyond the bottom rung of the ladder
        Despite the pains, bruises, tribulations,
        We are climbing these rungs
        The going sometimes is tough,
        Yet we continue to climb,

                                                top
                                      the
                            reach
                      until we
                one
        by
One

        Rising above the poverty that once entrapped us

        Rising to new and unimaginable heights

        Rising to positions of Authority,
        Of Responsibility,
        Of Accountability,
        Of Respectability,
        And of Unity,
        Using every avenue and door of opportunity.

Oceans of Love: To Us From Us

We're gonna take control of who we are,
What we do,
And what we can do.
We're gonna take control of our destiny.
We are here.

The hue of our skin may be different.
We cannot control that,
Nor is that a problem to us or for us.
We are here and I know
That we're gonna make it.
From here, I can clearly see…
We're gonna make it.

Dee Freeman

Oceans of Love: To Us From Us

FREEDOM: THE PRIZE

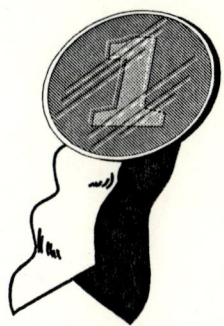

A people once enslaved should strive to rise; never, ever remain so.
As a people, we must put emphasis on the past, just so our youth will know,
That they are key to our race's most vital survival.
They must bare the cost-yes, it's high-for our desperately needed revival.

We need to wake up-check out the number of young men who are now jailed.
Look back a few hundred years and one might recognize a similarly brutal tale.
Enslaved <u>long</u> ago - taken from our Motherland - trapped, captured and incarcerated.
Enslaved <u>Now</u>! Not given equality on our shared land; deprived and openly degraded.

Dee Freeman

Enslaved <u>again</u>? We must take charge and loosen the powers of our enlightened minds.
We must not fall back into the traps of callousness of today's uncaring mankind.
Enslaved <u>again</u>? What people have the least wealth of this most powerful nation?
Can we survive the gangs and drugs to be represented in the future generations?

The enslavers are wagering, we'll buckle to this subtle and gross oppression.
But we, as a people, must stand up-make winning this battle our only obsession.
The act of slavery was theoretically banned countless years ago.
But, the jails and our financial condition, convince me, we yet have miles to go.

We can't let those few who would enslave us, win this dastardly and dehumanizing feat.
We must stand together, grow together and never accept such a defeat.
We must do as Maya Angelou encourages as she believes, "…and still I rise."
We can succeed, if we band together to make equality and **freedom our #1 prize**.

ABOUT THE AUTHOR

Dee Freeman, a native Arkansian, left the south during the sixties to follow her dream, which proved extremely elusive. Now, finally closing in on that dream, she happily immerses herself in her passion - writing. She provides *The Plexus* (a local newspaper, with distribution throughout Michigan) with its' poetry Korner. Her goal, to finish her first fiction novel before the end of 2002, is on track, as well as her planned series of *Poetry, She Wrote* books of inspiration, motivation and romance.

Delores thoroughly enjoys writing and sharing her poetry through presentations at special annual luncheons, for tributes honoring the leadership of community and churches, and at other functions held throughout Lansing and surrounding areas. She's had a number of poems published, and has plans to provide some lyrics for musical recordings. She sincerely hopes her words will benefit all who read them-gently touching, softly soothing, fervently healing, enthusiastically motivating, and delightfully awakening.

Delores, a former financial analyst for General Motors, resides in Lansing, Michigan with her husband, Myron, as their three children left the nest a number of years ago.

Printed in the United States
903100004B